...if you grew up with

George Washington

by RUTH BELOV GROSS

Pictures by JACK KENT

SCHOLASTIC BOOK SERVICES

NEW YORK · TORONTO · LONDON · AUCKLAND · SYDNEY · TOKYO

Many people helped me when I was writing this book. The 2nd- and 3rd-grade students in Mrs. Faye Friday's class at the Carr School in Dallas, North Carolina, told me what they wanted to know about George Washington's time. The librarians and staff of The New York Public Library, the library of Scholastic Inc., and the research library in Colonial Williamsburg were wonderfully helpful. The New York Public Library also generously allowed me to use the Frederick Lewis Allen Memorial Room.

For all these kindnesses, and for those of other specialists who are not named, my sincere thanks.

R.B.G.

ISBN 0-590-31608-7

Text copyright © 1982 by Ruth Belov Gross. Illustrations copyright © 1982 by Scholastic Inc. All rights reserved. Published by Scholastic Book Services, a division of Scholastic Inc.

12 11 10 9 8 7 6 5 4 3 2 1   1   2 3 4 5 6/8
Printed in the U.S.A.   07

*For Willy
and for Beatrice
with my love*

CONTENTS

If you grew up with George Washington, you would have lived a long time ago. George Washington was born in Virginia in the year 1732.

Virginia is a state now, in the southern part of the United States. But when George Washington was a boy, it was one of the colonies that belonged to England.

This book tells you what it was like to live in Virginia when George Washington was growing up there. That was in the 1730's and the 1740's.

The people who came to settle in the colonies were called colonists, and the times they lived in are called colonial times.

Here are some of the people you will be reading about in this book —

Farmers. Nearly all of the colonists in Virginia lived on farms and grew tobacco. Most of them owned just enough land to make a living. Some were very poor.

Planters. Rich farmers were usually called planters. They had lots of land and lots of slaves to work on it. Their farms were called plantations.

The richest planters lived in the eastern part of Virginia, close to the sea. That is where the Washington family lived. George Washington's father was not one of the very rich planters, but he was not poor either.

People in the back country. The western part of Virginia was called the back country. It was mostly wilderness.

Slaves. Slaves were brought from Africa and sold to the farmers and planters.

This book does not tell you anything about the people who lived in towns. There were only a few towns in Virginia when George Washington was growing up. Some of the towns had only four or five houses.

The biggest town in Virginia was Williamsburg, the capital. About two thousand people lived there.

Today, visitors can go to Williamsburg and see what it was like in colonial times.

What kind of house
did George Washington live in
when he was a little boy?

George Washington was born in a farm house. His family moved to another farm when he was three years old. They moved to a third farm when he was almost seven.

There were cows and pigs and chickens and dogs and horses on each farm. There were fields of corn and wheat and tobacco. And at the edge of the farm there was a river.

The houses that the Washingtons lived in are not there anymore, and nobody knows exactly what they looked like. They were probably ordinary farm houses.

They might have had four rooms downstairs and two rooms upstairs. They did not have bathrooms or kitchens in them.

Where was the cooking done?

The cooking was done in a separate building. It was warm in Virginia, and people liked to keep the heat of the kitchen away from the rest of the house.

Kitchens were hotter in those days than they are now, because all the cooking and baking was done in a big fireplace. Pots of food were hung over the fire or set in front of it on the hearth.

Some families did not have another building to cook in. Poor farmers and people in the back country lived in small cabins with

one or two rooms. They had to cook in the cabin, eat in it, and sleep in it.

Slave families lived in one-room cabins. They did not have separate kitchens either.

What about the bathroom?

In colonial times, the toilet was outside. It was in a special little house called the *necessary* house. People also called it a *privy*.

There was no special place for washing yourself or for taking a bath. When you wanted to get washed, you would just pour some water into a bowl. The colonists thought it was not healthy to wash themselves too much.

Some colonists did brush their teeth. They used twigs for toothbrushes, and they used salt and water instead of toothpaste.

George Washington brushed his teeth, but later on they had to be pulled out anyway. When he was President he had false teeth. Most people think they were made of wood, but they weren't. They were made out of the tusk of a hippopotamus.

How did people light the house at night?

Almost everyone used candles. Most people made their own candles, and they were careful not to use them up too fast. Even rich people tried not to waste candles.

The best candles were made from beeswax or from the tiny berries that grew on a bush called the bayberry bush. Bayberry candles had a nice smell when they burned.

Everyday candles were usually made out of sheep fat and ox fat. If bear grease or some other animal fat was handy, it was used too. Candles made from animal fat smelled bad and made a lot of smoke.

Poor people often burned pine knots in the fireplace. Pine knots were chunks of wood that came from pine trees. They burned brightly, but they also left a puddle of messy, sticky tar.

What did children do to have fun?

They played ball.
They flew kites.
They played marbles.
They spun tops.
They jumped rope.
They blew soap bubbles.
They went swimming.
They went fishing.
They rolled hoops.

They played with dolls.
They played with toy soldiers.
They played house.
They played with their pets.

They played leapfrog and hide and seek and blind man's buff.

They played and sang "London Bridge Is Falling Down" and "Here We Go Round the Mulberry Bush."

They went horseback riding.

They went to horse races.

And they sometimes played cards.

Children also had fun going to fish feasts and barbecues and fairs with their families.

Fish feasts and barbecues were big outdoor parties that lasted all day. At a barbecue, there was always roast pig to eat.

At fish feasts the men and boys went fishing. Then everybody ate fried fish.

Fairs usually lasted for two or three days. People came to buy and sell farm animals and to have a good time.

At a fair, there were prizes for wrestling and dancing and playing the fiddle. A man could win a prize for catching a greased pig, riding the slowest horse in a slow horse race, or whistling a tune without laughing.

Did they read books?

Children didn't read books for fun, the way they do now. There weren't many books that were fun to read.

How did grown-ups have fun?

What grown-ups liked best was to have parties, and dance, and get together with their friends and relatives.

They also liked to ride horses and have horse races and play cards and gamble and go hunting and fishing.

A visitor from England went to a wedding on a big plantation and wrote about it in his diary. He said that after the wedding everybody ate and danced for three days. They danced so hard that every lady wore out a pair of satin dancing slippers every night.

Parties often lasted for two or three days. The guests would stay and have a good time until everybody was tired and there wasn't much left to eat.

People in Virginia didn't wait for a wedding or a big party to visit each other. They loved to go visiting, and they went as often as they could.

A man from the next farm might drop in and stay for dinner. Or a cousin and his wife and their six children and four servants might drop in and stay for a week.

There were no telephones, so people didn't always know when company was coming. But that didn't matter. In Virginia, everyone loved having company as much as they loved to visit.

Even strangers were welcome. If you were traveling, you could stay overnight or have a meal at almost any house you came to. The people on the farms and plantations were glad to have someone new to talk to.

Where did visitors sleep?

Visitors slept anywhere there was room for them. Many houses had beds in the hall, beds in the dining room, and beds in the parlor. In those days, people weren't fussy about where they slept.

Some rich planters had very big houses with lots of beds. When they gave parties, they might have forty or fifty guests staying over. They put two or three guests in each bed. The others slept on thin mattresses on the floor.

Poor families often lived in one-room cabins. If they had a bed, everyone slept in it. If not, they all slept on the floor. When company came they just moved over.

When George Washington was seventeen years old, he went to the back country to measure some land. Along the way he stayed with many poor families. He told a friend about it in a letter.

He said he usually slept on the floor with the family. Everyone would lie down in front of the fire on a bearskin or on some straw — "like a parcel of dogs or cats," George said.

Would you go to school?

You might go to school, or you might not. There were not many schools in Virginia.

Rich parents sometimes sent their children to school in England. Some children were sent there when they were only six or seven years old. Boys went mostly, but a few girls were sent to England too.

Some rich children stayed in Virginia and went to school right in their own house. The teacher lived with the family and taught the children at home.

Sometimes a few farm families would get together and hire a teacher for their children. They might even build a little schoolhouse in an empty field near the farms. The minister might teach a few children too.

Slave children hardly ever had a chance to learn to read and write.

What kind of school
did George Washington go to?

Most likely George Washington went to a school near his farm. He probably went there from the time he was seven or eight years old until he was eleven or twelve — but nobody knows for sure.

What would you learn in school?

Farm children usually learned to read a little, write a little, and do some arithmetic. Boys were likely to go to school longer than girls, and they were more likely than girls to study arithmetic.

Rich boys needed a good education so they could go to college. They studied Greek and Latin and French and mathematics and

An apprentice had to work hard to learn a trade.

history and geography. Their sisters almost never studied those things. Girls weren't allowed to go to college.

What if you didn't go to school?

If you didn't go to school, your parents might teach you to read and write — if they knew how. Or when you were about fourteen, you might become an *apprentice*. Some children became apprentices when they were younger.

Being an apprentice meant you were sent to live with another family until you were grown up. You would promise to work for them, and they would promise to teach you.

Girl apprentices were taught to be good housewives, and boys were taught a trade.

Most boys also learned reading and writing and arithmetic, but a girl might only learn to read the Bible and to write her name.

Why didn't girls learn as much as boys?

People didn't think it made sense for girls to study a lot. Girls were supposed to get married when they were sixteen or seventeen years old. After that they were supposed to stay at home and keep house.

A girl who lived on a farm had to learn to spin and knit and sew when she was young. She had to learn to cook. And she had to learn how to do farm work.

Girls who lived on grand plantations had to learn other things — how to run a big house with lots of servants, how to give parties and balls, how to have fine manners.

Rich girls also learned to draw and embroider, play a musical instrument, and dance a minuet.

On a plantation, the boys took dancing lessons too. Dancing was one of the things that George Washington liked to do best.

What kind of food would you eat?

Most likely you would eat boiled rabbit, stewed squirrel, and pigeon pudding. If you lived in the back country, you would probably have stewed bear too.

You would eat deer meat and lots of ham and bacon. You would eat fish and chicken, beans and pumpkins, apples and peaches and berries.

There were no refrigerators then, and most things would spoil after a few days. So almost everything you ate had to be smoked, dried, pickled, salted, or cooked in sugar syrup to keep it from spoiling.

The Virginians were especially good at

making smoked ham. Smoked Virginia ham is still famous today.

Your parents would probably give you beer or wine or hard cider to drink. You would also drink some milk.

You would be sure to eat corn every day — corn bread and cooked hominy mostly.

Did everyone have enough to eat?

There was enough food for everybody. But only the rich people had a lot of fancy things to eat. Many poor families and people in the back country ate pork and hominy for dinner almost every day.

Slaves were usually given corn bread and the parts of the hog their owners didn't want. Most slaves also got some salted fish and some vegetables.

Very often slaves were allowed to grow a few extra vegetables and raise a few chickens of their own.

Would you have good manners when you ate?

Some people were fussy about manners, and some weren't.

A man who was visiting Maryland, a

colony near Virginia, wrote in his diary about the day a poor family invited him to dinner. The family had a wooden bowl with fish in it, and they just grabbed the fish with their hands.

"They used neither knife, fork, spoon, plate, or napkin," he said, "because, I suppose, they had none to use."

Most families did have something to use, though — a few spoons, at least, and a hunting knife. And many people had napkins for wiping their sticky fingers.

Forks were used mostly by rich people. They often had fine china dishes too. They were careful about the way they set the table and about the way they ate. Good manners were important to them.

When George Washington was fourteen or fifteen years old, he read a book called *Rules of Civility and Decent Behaviour in Company and Conversation*. The book had one hundred and ten rules for being polite.

George Washington must have liked the book, because he copied it all down in his own notebook.

"Put not your meat to your Mouth with your Knife," one rule said.

"Cleanse not your teeth with the Table Cloth Napkin Fork or Knife," another rule said.

Rule 98 said, "Drink not nor talk with your mouth full."

This is what George Washington's
handwriting looked like. The first rule says,
"Every Action done in company ought to be with Some Sign
of Respect of those that are Present."

What kind of clothes would you wear?

If your father was a rich planter, your clothes would be made out of silk and velvet and satin and the finest linens and cottons and woolens.

You might have a coat with gold lace on it, and shoes with silver buckles. Your fine clothes would come from England.

If you were poor, your father would probably make your shoes, and your mother would make your clothes.

All your clothes would be made out of rough, scratchy linen and rough, scratchy wool. Your shoes would be heavy and stiff, but you would wear them only in cold weather anyhow.

If you were a slave, you would wear the plainest and the poorest clothes of all. The planter who owned you would give you your clothes.

Every year the planter would give you a few new things to wear. But mostly your clothes would be old and raggedy.

Slaves who worked in the planter's house were called house servants. They usually got better clothes than the slaves who worked in the fields.

Where would you keep your clothes?

You would hang your clothes on wooden pegs or you would keep them in wooden chests. There weren't any clothes closets in colonial days.

What did little children wear?

Little girls wore long dresses — and so did little boys. Girls and boys were dressed almost exactly alike until they were about four or five years old.

When a boy was four or five, or maybe sooner, he stopped wearing dresses and began wearing *breeches*. Breeches were trousers that came to the knee.

On the day a boy got his first pair of breeches, people said he was *breeched*. From then on, he wore the kind of clothes that grown men wore.

When a girl was four years old she did not make a big change in the way she dressed. She was already wearing the kind of clothes that grown women wore.

It was too hot in Virginia to be dressed up
all the time. Around the house, everybody wore
more comfortable clothes. This man is wearing
a *banyan*. His son is wearing one too.
A banyan was something like a long bathrobe.

Rich girls and their mothers carried fans.
That was the fashion.

When they went outdoors, they often wore
long gloves and a mask. That was the
fashion too. They did not want their
arms and face to get suntanned.

When a lady went to a fancy party or a ball, she stuck the tiny bits of black silk on her face. The bits of silk were supposed to make her look more beautiful. They were shaped like moons or stars or circles and were called *beauty patches*.

Not everyone owned mirrors. They were expensive.

Most people wore a cap or a hat all the time, even in the house.

Everyone wore a cap to bed at night.

Babies wore caps day and night.

A sunbonnet helped to keep the sun off a little girl's face.

A planter's wife would wear a cap in the house most of the time.

When she went out, she would put a hat on top of her cap.

Planters usually shaved their hair off
and wore a wig instead. Young boys
sometimes wore wigs too.

Wigs were hot and itchy. When
a man took off his fancy clothes,
he was glad to take his wig off
and put on a cap.

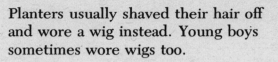

This is the kind of hat
most men wore.

Were there any Indians?

There were Indians in Virginia long before the English colonists lived there.

By the time George Washington was born, nearly all the Indians were in the western part of Virginia. So he did not see many Indians when he was growing up.

Most likely the Indians showed the first colonists how to grow corn and watermelons and sweet potatoes. The colonists learned from the Indians how to preserve pork by smoking it, how to make bread out of corn, and how to make medicines out of plants.

At times the Indians and the colonists were at war. When George Washington was in his twenties, he led a group of soldiers across the mountains to fight the Indians and the French in the French and Indian War.

How did people get around in Virginia?

Mostly they rode horses. Slaves did not have horses of their own, but just about everybody else did. There were no cars or trains or planes in those days.

The Virginia colonists loved horseback riding and would rather ride than walk. The Indians thought that was funny. They said the colonists were so lazy they needed six legs instead of two just to visit a neighbor.

On a long trip, a traveler would often take two horses — one to ride on and one for the baggage. You might ride through dark forests, across muddy streams, and over rocks. You could get lost in a swamp or caught in a storm.

It might take a whole day to go twenty or twenty-five miles.

Rich planters and their families often rode
in carriages that were pulled by horses.
Carriages cost a lot of money, and they could
be used only where the roads were good.

An ordinary farmer could not afford
a carriage. He used a wagon instead.

The finest plantations in Virginia were right on a river. If you lived on a river, you would probably visit friends and go to church in your family's sailboat or rowboat.

Travelers often had to take a ferry to get across a river or a creek or a stream.

The
FISH &
FOWL

Were there places to stay overnight when you were traveling?

Travelers in Virginia knew they could stop at almost any house they came to. Men could also stop at a tavern.

Taverns were often dirty. The food was often bad. And at night a man was likely to find some strangers snoring away in his room — and probably in his bed. So it was hard to get a good night's rest.

The best part about stopping at a tavern was the chance to meet people and find out what was happening in other parts of Virginia and in other colonies. Sometimes there might even be a traveler from England or France.

*Could you hear the news
on radio or TV?*

No. Radio and TV were not invented until about two hundred years after George Washington was born.

Just a few years after George Washington was born, though, a man in Williamsburg started the first newspaper in Virginia. His paper was called *The Virginia Gazette*. It came out once a week.

Williamsburg was the biggest town in Virginia. The people who lived there could read the newspaper as soon as it came out. In other parts of the colony, people had to wait until special messengers on horseback could bring it to them.

How did people get their mail?

When you had a letter to send, you would take it to the nearest tavern and put it on a table. In a tavern, people were always coming and going. If someone was going in the right direction, he would probably take your letter with him.

I'M GOING THAT WAY!

The traveler might not be going exactly where your friend lived.

But at last your friend
would get the letter.

When George Washington was still very young, a post office was opened in Virginia. But for many years the post office wasn't much help in getting the mail around. People still thought that the best way to mail a letter was to leave it at a tavern.

What kind of money
did people use in Virginia?

Sometimes the people used English money — pounds and shillings and pence. There wasn't much English money around, though.

Sometimes they used money from other countries. They used gold and silver coins from Spain and France and Portugal. There wasn't a lot of that money around, either.

Most of the time the people in Virginia used tobacco instead of money. There was plenty of tobacco in Virginia. Everyone knew they could send tobacco to England and sell it. So having tobacco was as good as having money.

You could buy a horse with tobacco. You could pay the doctor with tobacco. You could pay your taxes with it. And if you broke a law and had to pay a fine, you could pay the fine with tobacco.

If you killed a wolf around your farm, you would get fifty or one hundred pounds of tobacco as a reward.

How did people carry their tobacco around?

People did not drag barrels of tobacco around with them. They didn't have to. All they needed was a special piece of paper that said the tobacco was in a warehouse.

As long as you kept the piece of paper, the tobacco was yours. As soon as you gave the paper to someone else, the tobacco belonged to that person.

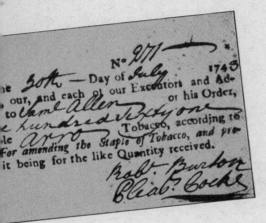

This tobacco certificate says that the tobacco is in a warehouse. The certificate could be used instead of money.

Who made the laws for the colony?

The people of Virginia made their own laws. But the King of England could veto any law he didn't like.

The laws were made in the town of Williamsburg. Every two years, the voters in each county picked two people to go to Williamsburg and help make the laws.

Election time was like a holiday. Just before the election, the people who wanted to get elected would give parties for the voters.

Then, on election day, the voters would gather at the court house in their county. They came to see their old friends, to hear the latest news, to have fun, and to vote.

When it was a person's turn to vote, he

walked up to a long table. The sheriff would be sitting at the table, and so would the people who wanted to be elected.

"And how do you vote, sir?" the sheriff would ask.

In a voice that everybody could hear, the voter would call out the name of the man he was voting for.

The man would stand up and bow. Then he would say something like this: "Thank you, sir. As long as I live I will treasure your vote in my memory."

People crowded around so they could see who was winning the election and who was losing. They would shout when they liked a vote, and they would boo when they didn't.

After the election, the winners were expected to give another party.

Did everyone vote?

No. Children couldn't vote. Women couldn't vote. Indians couldn't vote. Slaves couldn't vote. The only people who were allowed to vote in Virginia were white men who owned land.

Did a man have to be rich to own land?

No. Land did not cost a lot of money in those days.

Did a man have to be rich to get elected?

There was no law that said a man had to be rich to get elected. But all the men who were elected were rich. It was the custom in Virginia to have rich men run the colony.

What were some of the laws in Virginia?

One law said that people in Virginia had to go to church. Even so, many people didn't go unless they felt like it. Sometimes they went to church just to see their friends.

It was against the law to swear. Gambling was not against the law, but it was against the law for people to cheat or fight when they gambled.

Another law said that people had to keep their pigs and goats from running loose in town.

People were usually punished when they broke a law. Sometimes they had to pay a fine. Sometimes they got a whipping. If they murdered somebody, or if they stole a horse, they might be put to death.

*Did they have doctors
when George Washington
was a young boy?*

Yes. But there weren't many doctors. In those days, there were no schools in the colonies where you could learn to be a doctor.

A boy who wanted to be a doctor usually left home and went to live in a doctor's house. He watched the doctor and helped him. By the time he was twenty-one years old he could call himself a doctor.

There were some fake doctors too. These were people who said they had all kinds of secret ways to cure anything.

Mostly, though, people in Virginia took care of themselves when they were sick. Many families had a book called *Every Man his own Doctor*. They would read the book and do what it told them to do.

On most plantations, the planter or his wife would take care of anyone who was sick or got hurt.

What happened when you got sick?

If you got sick, your mother or your father or the doctor would try to make you feel better. But some of the things they did for you would make you feel worse.

They might give you water mixed with the bark of a tree. The bark was supposed to cure chills and fevers. It tasted bitter and made you sweat.

They might give you *Indian Physick*. Indian Physick was supposed to cure almost everything. It made you throw up.

And of course you might get castor oil.

If the castor oil and Indian Physick and tree bark didn't fix you up, you might get a hot, wet cloth on your head or chest or stomach. The medicine on the cloth would make blisters on your skin.

If you were *still* sick, someone might come and take some blood out of one of your veins. That was called *bleeding*. Most people in colonial days thought bleeding was good for you.

One nice thing you might get when you were sick was chicken soup.

Many babies and children died, though. Two of George Washington's sisters died before he was eight years old.

Babies and children died because no one knew about germs in those days. They did not know it was important to have clean food and water. They did not have shots to keep children from getting sick or the medicines we have to make people well.

But George Washington lived a long and healthy life. When he was fifty-seven years old he became the first President of the United States.

He was President for eight years. Then he went home to Mount Vernon, his beautiful plantation in Virginia. He died there in 1799. He was sixty-seven years old.

Other books by Ruth Belov Gross

Alligators and Other Crocodilians
A Book About Benjamin Franklin
A Book About Christopher Columbus
A Book About Pandas
A Book About Your Skeleton
The Bremen-town Musicians
Dangerous Adventure! Lindbergh's Famous Flight
The Emperor's New Clothes
Hansel and Gretel
If You Were a Ballet Dancer
The Laugh Book
Money, Money, Money
The Mouse's Wedding
Snakes
True Stories About Abraham Lincoln
What Do Animals Eat?
What Is That Alligator Saying? A science book about
the way animals talk to each other